Surviving the Call of God

Getting more out of God

So God can get more out of you

Lessons and devotions

For the "Called of Christ"

Copyrighted Material

Copyright © 2024
Date of publication January 2024
Authored by Dr. Derrick Lamont Randolph Sr.
Published by Journey of Faith Ministries
Baltimore, Maryland
United States of America

The character illustrations are works-for-hire.

All concepts, ideas, copy, sketches, art work, electronic files and other materials related to the Journey of Faith are the property of Journey of Faith Ministries.

Journey of Faith Ministries
contact@journeyoffaithministries.org
www.journeyoffaithministries.org

All rights reserved.
This book may not be reproduced in whole or in part by any process without written permission from the copyright holder.

ISBN-13: 978-1-944166-04-5

Table of Contents

Part 1 - Introduction 6

Part 2 – Three (3) Important Lessons 7

   It's too much for you at first 8

   Learn their lessons, but be yourself 9

Part 3 – Eight (8) Dead Ends 10

   1) *Impersonation* 10

   2) *Indifference* 11

   3) *Arrogance* 12

   4) *Ego* 13

   5) *Abuse* 14

   6) *Fear* 15

   7) *Resistance* 16

   8) *Forgetfulness* 17

Part 4 – Three (3) Do(s) 18

   i. *Be unique* 18

   ii. *Change with the times* 19

   iii. *Be a part of something bigger than you* 20

Part 5 – Two (2) Don'ts 21

   i. *Don't run from the pain* 21

   ii. *Don't blame anyone else* 22

Part 6 – A word of Encouragement 23

   "Obey God" 23

Part 7 – Eight (8) Points from Peter's Call 28

   2. The Point is...Jesus will interrupt your comfort zones 30

   3. The Point is...Jesus will reign in your context 31

   4. The Point is...Jesus will perform a miracle to reform your faith 31

   5. The Point is...Jesus will empowered you 32

6. The Point is...Jesus will appoint you to a place & put you in it............ 32

8. The Point is...Jesus will call you to wrestle with your faith 33

Part 8 – Twenty Five (25) Tools in the Minister's Toolkit 34

"Relationships with People" 34

"Pastoral Care & Visitations" 35

"Healing & Deliverance" 35

"Sowing & Reaping" 35

"Preaching & Teaching" 35

"Disciplines" 36

"Spiritual Maintenance" 37

"Loving" 38

"Long Suffering" 38

"Growing" 38

"Finding Balance" 39

"Longevity" 39

Part 9 - What you need to survive the call 40

Part 10 - You need to Testify 77

Part 11 – Reminder to Survive the Call 81

Part 1 - Introduction

Receiving the call of God is such a unique experience. It is as if God invades your life and extends an invitation to try a new life. God may reveal His call and will for your life in a brief moment of time. God may reveal a little at a time over a lifetime. Either way, the experience is personal, memorable and outright extraordinary.

It is easy to lose yourself in the experience of hearing the call. Once you are sure you've got it, all earthly pleasure and glory pale in comparison to the treasure you've found. God's will is sometimes a mystery, that's hidden behind your quest to find it, but when you have heard God speak, felt God move, or sensed God directing or shifting the course of your life, you will begin to see behind the veil and know emphatically what you were created for. When you arrive at this place it is both liberating and daunting. On one hand, you've conquered the wilderness fog and found the path to your destiny. On the other hand, you're on day 1 of an impossible mission. You have no instruction manual for surviving the call of God. There is no law for arriving at the place of purposeful fulfilment. There is no set of 10 commandments, no great commandment, no roadmap, or plan to help you survive the journey of your call and help you live worthy of the call. There is no standard operating procedure to help you walk in your call until you've completed your assignment. You will have to trust God! I plead to you, trust God and He will lead you each step of the way. Your journey will lead you in many directions, through many experiences to learn, grown and become anew. Why, because we are called to follow Jesus Christ and to live a new life in him.

Part 2 – Three (3) Important Lessons

Transformation Takes Time

If you are following God in pursuit of a calling on your life, please take a minute and thank God that His grace is there to guide you. Believe it or not, you are on a journey. It takes time to get there, and there are many traps to block you, but God's grace will guide you.

Look at the apostle Paul; he said "that he was called by God to proclaim Christ among the Gentiles (Gal. 1:15–16; cf. Rom. 1:1)." [2] It took time for an outrageous and zealous Pharisee who persecuted the church to be transformed into an apostle and leader of the church. Paul had a great role and function in the church, but he had to undergo great transformation to get there. Trust me, manifestation of the call may take a while, but the transformation is ongoing.

Transformation takes a lifetime. It doesn't stop when you find your role or function in the church. For example, the call to preach is about more than just preaching. The call to preach, teach, sing, dance, lead, help, and heal others is a call to become! You will become more than just a person that provides the ministerial function. You are called to go on a journey and become the person God had in mind before He created you. A call to preach includes preaching but you will become far more than just a preacher. A dancer masters his or her moves, but a dancer must first commit to taking a journey with God. On that journey you will experience sanctification and find eternal salvation in the Lord. My point is that there's no end for you to focus and settle on, but God.

Commit to your journey with God. Learn and grow as you go. You will become like Christ. But by all means, don't lock on the temporary role, function, job, title, gift, anointing, praise and glory that you get to experience on the way. To survive the call, we must remember to focus on the God of the call and stay on the journey to eternal transformation. Else, the glamor of the call will lead you astray.

It's too much for you at first

The biggest 'Call' lesson that I've learned is that in the moment that God calls you, your assignment is truly too much to handle. You will feel unprepared and unequipped for it. It will appear impossible, but God will grant you a season of preparation and consecration before your assignment begins. So, don't worry. If you trust God, you will be ready.

You will get to know and serve the God that has called you. This time of preparation will allow you to receive the revelation of God and develop your personal relationship with God. You will join the church in service and fellowship. You will serve the body of Christ and seek the edification of your brothers and sisters in the faith. You will pursue their growth and maturity. Getting through the call to your place of destiny takes time. Remember it's too much at first. Prepare to get to know God, join the church in service in fellowship and seek the edification of your brethren.

Learn their lessons, but be yourself

So often, we watch and study those who have successfully gone before us in the area that we're called to serve. Until we gain the confidence we need, we emulate their walk, talk, style, method, persona and behaviors if we can. I've discovered the key to watching others. We should watch, listen, learn and question them so that we can learn from their experiences, but we must maintain our own personality, develop our own character in Christ, and establish our own trust in God with our calling. God wants to use you. He wants your spirit, soul, and mind. God wants to use the gifts, and abilities He placed in you. God invested in you and He wants to draw from the experiences, expertise, and expressions of faith that are emerging in you.

Every time God has called me to do something great, I expected to start right away. Of course it never happened. Now I understand that God warns us with His calling. When God calls us, we aren't ready yet. God knows. He has all knowledge and wisdom. He calls us to Himself, to get prepared and then God sends us out on assignment. Though we're not qualified when God calls us, when it's time to go, God will have us prepared.

Now, let's look at some dead ends, some do(s), don't(s), points from Peter, encouragement and tools you need to survive the journey as you follow your call from God.

Part 3 – Eight (8) Dead Ends

As you navigate the maze of your journey, avoid these dead ends!

1) *Impersonation*

Have you ever noticed when someone is new on the scene that they start out emulating the person they admire most? You can tell by the way they look, act, walk, and talk. That's because they've only struggled with their craft on the surface level. Their commitment hasn't been challenged yet. They were talented enough to make it but they haven't been frustrated with the process yet. If you've ever paid your dues working at something, and put your time in, you will come to a point where the people, process, and things you have to endure will frustrate you and make you want to quit. You will vacillate back and forth until you eventually give in, dig in, and deal with the part of it that bothers you. Only then will you be yourself, with all of your hurt and pain, frustration and disdain, in what you do, how you feel, and in how you relate to others. There's nothing like watching someone who has a heavy heart, give the performance, play the game, sing the song of their career. It's the same with ministry. There's nothing like seeing someone who has been going through, finally minister to others who are going through. That's transparency. That's growth. There's no room for imitating, anymore. That is what you want to work toward.

Early on, embrace your fascination. Enjoy your excitement. Embrace the honeymoon. The rush of emotion will magnify all that you do for God. Likewise, when you are going through the rough season, embrace the pain. Welcome the feelings of frustration. Be honest if you are contrite. As you serve out of the pain, and follow the call when you are frustrated, you will be pulling from out of your pain. You will be unknowingly relating to what others feel. The combination of the presence of the Holy Spirit and the humanity of your experience makes a powerful impact on all who experience your ministry.

2) *Indifference*

Over time, your commitment to the call will develop you. The process will transform you into the person God is calling you to be. All of it works together to mature you spiritually. Several things will occur as you commit more to the call. You will submit to a form of leadership, develop a system of accountability, and develop a greater measure of character. The signs of growth will be all over you. That alone is greater than the destination you have in mind. My advice to you is to be yourself right where you are. Find out where God has given you authority and find out what is your domain. Then be present right where you are. Be, e.g. exist, live, thrive, be relational, functional, and masterful right there in your domain. Be influential for God and for God's kingdom right where you are. Be honest, accountable and real in your domain. Be connected, accessible, and consistently available to others. Ask if you've been helpful. Find out if you are relatable. If not, work on it. They don't need you to preach at them, lecture them, perform for them, and exercise self-centered authority over them. No, people need to be in relationship with you. They need the real you. They need the humble novice, who longs to be a master but is comfortable being around masters for now. Trust me, you can't be yourself and impersonate someone else if you are going to be present with them. Be yourself and grow with those God has called you to serve with. They need the real you. You both deserve it.

3) Arrogance

How many of us have seen a measure of success, felt accomplished in our pursuits and then suffered and fell to that dead end of arrogance. You know becoming a public success can really go to our heads. Let me challenge you with this question, who do you think you are? Are you person that has submitted to eh will of God? If so, do you know that God turns over his children to an earthly form of leadership to facilitate your growth and development? Whether you are a leader or follower, you will have to submit yourself to someone else's leadership and authority for the benefit of accountability. Remember that Jesus, the Christ, our example, was submitted to the father. He was submissive to the will of His father, as revealed in the Lord's Prayer, when Jesus prayed, thy will be done. Then in the garden of Gethsemane, Jesus said, "not as I will, but as you will." Remember that your calling will bring you success and good fortune. You will naturally want to take the reins and direct your own path, leading you to the future you have in mind. I warn you that it only leads to pride, which leads to the great fall. Avoid the trap of arrogance. God has more in store for you but it is only reserved for the humble in spirit. Take breaks from your labor and yield to God. Thank God for your success and remind God that He is in charge. Yield to Him for further direction. It will save you from steering off course. God is calling and you don't know the path. Only God does!

4) Ego

There is a dead end called Ego. It lives in the talented. It lives in leaders. It lives in the disenfranchised. Your status, class, success or popularity neither excludes you from it nor guarantees you will suffer from it. One of the ways it effects the called is that it births totalitarianism that is the desire to take total control over others. Sometimes the called, chosen and favored will want to maintain the perks, power and pleasure of their newfound status by ruling with absolute power over others. It's easy when you have the calling, anointing, success and visible presence of God on your life to assume and exercise authority over those you serve with. You may gain control but you will unknowingly operate in it without God's leading. The problem with this behavior is that rulers have to be subject to God. Biblical records show that Pharaohs and Kings learned it. Soldiers and officers have learned it. God has always provided prophets to warn those in authority not to misuse or abuse their power. As you journey in the call of God, remember it will take a humble, yet keen servant to see ego at work and to stand up against it, whether it is in you or ruling over you. You will want to conquer it when you spot it. Get in posture now. Bow before the master, so you have the spiritual strength to stand up against the enemy. It's your call. Don't get caught in this dead end.

5) *Abuse*

Be watchful, prayerful and careful about abuse as well. Abusers can be outright cruel or subtly violent toward their people. Abuse allows one person to maintain power and privilege at the expense of others. Abusers devalue their victims, while treasuring the privilege they enjoy. King David abused his power, because untamed greed lived in his heart. David later repented because the prophet confronted and convicted him. On the journey, you will need the integrity and conviction of heart to test yourself.

6) Fear

The Pharisees in the New Testament abused their power as religious leaders. Jesus said that not only would they not enter the kingdom of God, they blocked others from entering and when they made a proselyte, they'd make him a devil just like them. You are not only called to avoid the trap of abuse, as a responsible servant, like Moses, you are called to stand up to the abusive and declare the will of God, that God wants men and women to live free and worship Him. Only a servant that is focused on God will have the courage and strength to stand up against those in authority who abuse their power. You will be an outcast; you will be treated unfavorably when you do so. You will however, be honored by God and privileged to serve another day.

Many are afraid to stand for Jesus and to acknowledge God publicly. Pilate denied his power and didn't make a decision when he had the chance. Peter denied his power at the outer courts (e.g. in the world). Don't be afraid of what the call presents. Many have become so afraid that they never fulfill even the first part of the assignment. The journey will teach you to overcome the spirit of fear. You must be willing to use each situation as an opportunity to overcome the crippling effects of fear. Dethrone it once and for all; face the challenge of fear. Even if you afraid, proceed as planned and serve God, but don't let it stop you.

A note to preachers…God needs faithful servants, not violent rulers. I challenge you to function as both a prophet and a priest. Go to God in prayer on behalf of others. Then wait for a prophetic word from God. That's what you will proclaim to the people. Trust me, you will never become a prophet if your ultimate goal is to excite or impress the people.

You will never develop the sincerity, care, concern or empathy to go to God on behalf of the people if you are abusive toward them or are afraid of them. This is a tough task. You have to gird up your loins and become one with the people if you want to serve them. A determined servant will be able to go to God in prayer on behalf of the people to receive a word. Remember that prayer and word go together. Courage and empathy work together also! Be strong and caring.

7) *Resistance*

Another encounter you'll face is the need for mentorship to help you. First, you need a relationship with God to help you. There are several groups that will miss the mark here. For starters, some of us will stop here, wanting God alone to guide you, teach and correct you. There is another group that will only want the help of the pastor, believing that the Pastor is the only human sufficient to help them along the journey. This group misses the mark as well. Others only want to learn from scripture. They don't trust the faithful leaders that God appoints. They don't value their wisdom or experience. The last group is the ones that can only learn from individuals in their local church, or our denomination, believing that all others are wrong, are erring in scripture and are incapable of adequately ministering to us. Others, sexually discriminate believing, we cannot learn from, listen to or take direction from women. All of these groups are missing the mark in terms of mentorship. Surviving the call of God takes surrender to others. Trust me; they will help you find your way.

8) Forgetfulness

Note to preachers…I've seen preachers choose the academy over the church. Some believe we are no longer in the church age, no longer required to submit to the authority of God's holy church. As a called, preacher of the gospel, you have to remember that you are still a member of the Lord's church. Whether you are an elder, minister or seminarian, you must understand that seminary is for developing scholars and contributing to scholarship. The church is the school for Christians and the training ground for ministers of the gospel.

Typically the church produces ministers of the gospel, who evangelize the lost and edify the body of Christ. Meanwhile, the seminary produces scholars whose research contributes to the secular and sacred libraries of time. It's great when a minister is able to get academic training for ministry in the seminary then contribute to academia with research. Ministers must remember to stay anchored with their connection to the church! No person is bigger than the church. You must cherish your relationship with the church. Serve it! Serve with it to make it better. God loves the church. You should honor God with your love, unity, and commitment to the church. He will honor you.

Part 4 – Three (3) Do(s)

i.   Be unique

We are all expected to develop private intimate relationships with Lord. Yet, when we get together as a church, we praise and worship the Lord together, publicly. We celebrate the Lord together, in public displays of praise. On the other hand, we enter into intimate worship together. In a sense, we are all going into our private spaces, sharing our private selves with others as we worship the Lord together. What we do in our private time with God is brought into the community, our local church and is offered collectively to God. We stand together in corporate worship, but each one of us is seeking the Lord, waiting for a personal touch, a rhema word, a revelation sent from God, tailor made for each of us. As we seek God and inquire of His will, remember that we are still clay in the potter's hands, forgiven for the things we struggled with and healed from the wounds and blemishes inflicted upon us. Remember that God can and will do the unthinkable to and for each of us, to enrich our lives. Our lives will never be identical. They will never transform us into the same likeness. We will walk, talk and act different. Welcoming the change in you, the difference made by your personality, will help you value yourself, your worth and the experience that God has given you. Enjoy who you are becoming.

ii. *Change with the times*

Understand that the times change, but our purpose as the church remains the same. I remember when I used to keep sermon notes in a notebook that I could periodically flip through to glean revelatory treasures in my quiet time. Now I keep notes in a computer file on my iPad. When I write sermon notes, I figure out which ones I will tweet to the world and share the bits of guidance that the Lord transmitted to me through the preacher's sermon. I still review that file periodically during my quiet time. I can also review my social media tweets, posts and blogs, to gather insight from past sermons. It is amazing how times change and methods change, but basic truths remain. We still need to hear from God. We still must grow as Christians. We are called to various assignments, places of authority, servant responsibilities, and to sufferings, but we will forever need our God and depend on our God. Let the times changes, but maintain your humble posture in Christ and forever depend on Him.

iii.   Be a part of something bigger than you

Remember that what you do affects the big picture. Small cogs turn into larger ones. You are a spirit member in the spirit world and your prayer adds to the warfare. You are but a soldier, striking small blows against the enemy. You may never realize your significance, but remember that when the war is over, and the kingdom of God celebrates, our roar is increased by our voice. Likewise, know that the small blows against the kingdom of darkness that you strike today, when combined with countless others, cumulates in a knockout punch that gives God the ultimate glory. Similar to a boxer's punch, the bicep alone will not knockout the competitor. It takes the force of the feet, ankle and leg muscles to steady the lower body on the ground, combined with the core, stomach, back, and thigh and muscles to sustain the body, along with the upper check, shoulder, biceps, triceps, and neck muscles to create the force needed to knock out the opponent. Consider yourself a muscle that creates the synergy to knock down the force of the enemy, to knock down the kingdom of darkness, to advance the kingdom of God for the eternal celebration and life of peace awaiting you. Don't despise small beginnings, slow starts, late blooming, background assignments, voiceless tasks, and invisible parts. All parts are needed. Each one leads to another. Your next assignment will be greater than the last. Lastly, whatever you do for Christ is major!

Part 5 – Two (2) Don'ts

i.   Don't run from the pain

You want a little pleasure but you need a little pain to make you strong!

As you prepare yourself to live out your calling and turn it into a being, remember that it is not a luxury. It is a suffering privilege to do so. Train yourself for the journey. Give yourself the pain of discipline along the way. Discipline yourself daily. Rather than seek pleasure, allow pleasure to be received as a grace given by God. Allow pleasure to be provided in due season. You will enjoy pleasure at a deeper level when you welcome it as a refreshing from the stress and strain of hard work. As the big eater chooses to eat to live rather than live to eat, so I plead with you to use pleasure to establish and maintain balance in your life, versus living your life for balance.

ii. *Don't blame anyone else*

Be careful not to play the blame game. Know that your current situation is your training ground. Though you are called, if you are a parent, you are commanded by God to shepherd and nurture your family. I warn you, don't sin against God by neglecting your family so you can minister in the church. So many of us will overlook our current situation and go searching for something beyond the horizon. I warn you, don't overlook your current situation. God plants you in a place to help you develop and later prove your mettle where you are. Right where you are, God wants you to be faithful over a few things. Grow in your faithful commitment to the small things. Don't just do stuff to pass the times. Be in the moment where you are. Be yourself. Be content where you are. Keep your focus on God. Wait for the word and revelation of God to show you what part of your life to focus on and develop next. While you are there, continue to celebrate your call, it's like celebrating your salvation. Grace to you.

Part 6 – A word of Encouragement

"Obey God"

Let's take a look at Psalm 119 for a word of encouragement. To survive the call of God, you must obey God! Verses 21-26 of Psalm 119 read, "You rebuke the <u>arrogant</u>, who are <u>accursed</u>, those who <u>stray</u> from your commands. Remove from me their <u>scorn</u> and <u>contempt</u>, for I keep your <u>statutes</u>. Though rulers sit together and <u>slander</u> me, your servant will <u>meditate</u> on your <u>decrees</u>. Your <u>statutes</u> are my delight; they are my <u>counselors</u>. I am <u>laid low</u> in the dust; <u>preserve</u> my life according to your word. I gave an <u>account</u> of my ways and you <u>answered</u> me; <u>teach</u> me your decrees."

Background (Sin & Obedience)

In William Barclay's, "The Mind of Jesus," the Early Christian philosopher, Senecca, declared that "Men love their vices and hate them at the same time. Man oscillates between right and wrong, unable to declare boldly and unequivocally for either. Man is not quite free, nor yet quite in bondage to the faults which [are] feared and hated." Man is "in an uncomfortable state, neither well nor ill; it "a weakness of the mind that sways between the two". "Things disturb [men], though they do not alter [their] principles." "[We] fall back into a life of leisure, only to be pricked to the will…by reading some brave words or seeing some fine example" On one hand, we are a helpless sinner, and at the same time, an adopted child of God, but Jesus saw in us a sleeping hero that could obey God and be great!

In the NT, the most common word for sin was hamartia. It was a shooting word that means a missing of the target; it is missing the target at which life must aim and hit.

The Problem

Unfortunately for us, many missed small targets will equal a life that misses the mark. The problem with sin is that, God called us to a certain life, and when we sin we fall into a habitual lifestyle of seeing, believing, thinking, saying and doing that steers us in the wrong direction. But God wants our lifestyle to line up with our calling in Christ. When we are called, we will get to the place of calling, and if our lifestyle don't line up with the calling, we will grieve and want to do better. We will eventually push ourselves to live appropriately for God. The problem is that no matter how hard we try, we can't get there alone.

God has to lead us into the place where we are living properly for God, in a committed relationship. Faith gets us into the relationship, but obedience keeps us there. God will teach us obedience. God will teach us to obey God's word. God instructs us to seek God's face. God's face is seen in the Word. When we look into the word, we see God and find out what God requires of us. Our relationship with God can be defined by our approach to God's word.

Confronting yourself

Are you in or out? When was the last time you let the word of God minister to your spirit and meet you at your point of need? If the pendulum of obedience swings between 2 distant ends, humility and arrogance, where are you? Do you know where you are? What defines your relationship to God's word? Are you arrogant or humble?

The main point is that God will preserve your life if you obey His word. He will preserve you, but He wants you humbly obedient. You can't get this guarantee from God until you become spiritually humble before God. You will never reach this place of humility until you know where you are on the scale of humility.

Know where you are in God

The arrogant stray from God's commands. The writer says that the arrogant holds god's people in contempt. If you are the one God considers arrogant and proud of yourself rather than in reverence of God, then know though you hold others in scorn and contempt, it's you that's held in god's scorn and contempt. The arrogant can't help but stray! The arrogant are rebuked; they stray from God's commands. They are accursed, held in scorn, and contempt. To keep from becoming arrogant, know that you have to go through!

The Solution - "Go through"

Be willing and ready to go through some things" It's what makes us faithful and righteous. The scripture says that the humble stay in the statues of God. The humble keep the statutes of God. They get slandered by rulers. They meditate on God's decrees. They delight in God's statutes, they see statues as counselors, they are laid low and they give an account of themselves and their behavior.

If you don't know where you are, ask God. David said I gave an account of my ways and you answered me. Wherever you are, God will help you because God has a plan for your life. Here's how. God preserves according to God's word. God answers [your prayers]. God teaches His decrees to us. Let's retell the scripture based on the insights we know!

Encouragement

Here is a little hope to help you. If you are on the wrong side of the pendulum, and humility is far from you, don't fret. Failure may eventually birth success. Yes, failure will help you see your true commitment. When we fail, fall short and miss the mark, then we will see our true level of commitment. When we fail, we also see who or what we are truly committed to.

Moreover, when we replace our hearts' commitment with a commitment to the word of God, we can finally return to our place in God, where God is perfect, and we fall short, but God uses grace to help us! Remember that it is your obedience to God that will help you survive the

Call! The Lord Jesus, the Christ, died on Calvary's cross, sacrificing Himself and His life to redeem you to God, so that you can enjoy an eternally enduring life with God. In this life with God, you will be called. It is your responsibility to survive the Call of God. If you live in disobedience you may be destroyed in it. My plea to you is to learn obedience to the Lord Jesus Christ and survive the Call of God.

Part 7 – Eight (8) Points from Peter's Call

Peter preached on the day of Pentecost, after 3 years of journeying with Jesus. For Jesus it was three years' worth of discipleship. For us, it may take many years to accomplish and accumulate that amount of experience, to witness that much ministry, and to develop the discipline, conviction and commitment. Let's revisit Peter's call. Let's sit at Peter's feet and learn how to survive the call of God.

One day John [the Baptist] was with "two of his disciples. When he saw Jesus passing by, he said, "Look, the Lamb of God!" When the two disciples heard him say this, they followed Jesus. Turning around, Jesus saw them following and asked, "What do you want?" They said, "Rabbi" (which means "Teacher"), "where are you staying?" "Come," he replied, "and you will see." So they went and saw where he was staying, and they spent that day with him. It was about four in the afternoon. Andrew, Simon Peter's brother, was one of the two who heard what John had said and who had followed Jesus. The first thing Andrew did was to find his brother Simon and tell him, "We have found the Messiah" (that is, the Christ). And he brought him to Jesus. Jesus looked at him and said, "You are Simon son of John. You will be called Cephas" (which, when translated, is Peter). (John 1:35b-42)

The point and purpose of this story is that your calling in Christ is the result of someone else's ministry. Someone else labored in the spirit, word and in prayer to draw you to Christ. John the Baptist's ministry drew Simon Peter in.

1. The Point is...You are someone else's fruit

According to the Gospel of Matthew, *"As Jesus was walking beside the Sea of Galilee, he saw two brothers, Simon called Peter and his brother Andrew. They were casting a net into the lake, for they were fishermen. "Come, follow me," Jesus said, "and I will send you out to fish for people." At once they left their nets and followed him."(Matthew 4:18)*

The point is that the call of God will interrupt you, e.g. your life, your will, your plans, your vocation, your desires, etc. Jesus told them to "Come, follow me." They left and followed Jesus, on the spot. Interpret this both literally and figuratively. They literally stopped what they were doing and left to follow Jesus to go where he went, to do what he said, to hear his words, follow his teachings. They figuratively left their state of being, state of mind and state of spiritual separation from God to follow Jesus and inquire into this new life, new purpose that Jesus had for them, and new status as citizens of the kingdom. They would soon discover what it meant to fish for people.

2. *The Point is…Jesus will interrupt your comfort zones*

Luke tells Peter's calling from a different perspective.

One day as Jesus was standing by the Lake of Gennesaret, the people were crowding around him and listening to the word of God. He saw at the water's edge two boats, left there by the fishermen, who were washing their nets. He got into one of the boats, the one belonging to Simon, and asked him to put out a little from shore. Then he sat down and taught the people from the boat. When he had finished speaking, he said to Simon, "Put out into deep water, and let down the nets for a catch." Simon answered, "Master, we've worked hard all night and haven't caught anything. But because you say so, I will let down the nets." When they had done so, they caught such a large number of fish that their nets began to break. So they signaled their partners in the other boat to come and help them, and they came and filled both boats so full that they began to sink. When Simon Peter saw this, he fell at Jesus' knees and said, "Go away from me, Lord; I am a sinful man!" For he and all his companions were astonished at the catch of fish they had taken, and so were James and John, the sons of Zebedee, Simon's partners. Then Jesus said to Simon, "Don't be afraid; from now on you will fish for people." So they pulled their boats up on shore, left everything and followed him. (Luke 5:1-12)

Jesus got into Peter's boat. Then he sat down and taught the people from the boat. Here, Jesus got into Peter's context, ministered to the people from where Peter was.

3. *The Point is...Jesus will reign in your context*

Jesus then performs a miracle in Peter's context. Peter couldn't accomplish what usually works for him. In that moment, Jesus provided a miracle for Peter, and convicted Peter for his lack of faith in Jesus. Peter realized he needed to trust in Jesus but didn't. Peter saw his frailty, his sinfulness, his emptiness all at once.

4. *The Point is...Jesus will perform a miracle to reform your faith*

Jesus reigns in every context. We must recognize His power over every situation. His power is never hindered, never withheld, never short-circuited. Jesus reigns over all creation!

Jesus gave Peter the healing, faith, spiritual power, and affirmation he needed. For, Jesus healed Peter's mother-in-law (Matthew 8:14). He called Peter to get out of the boat and to walk on the water (Matthew 14:29). Jesus confirmed Peter's revelation from God that Jesus was "the Messiah, the Son of the living God." He empowered Peter, strengthened his personal life and blessed Peter will the tools needed for a strengthened faith.

5. *The Point is...Jesus will empowered you*

Jesus also put Peter in his place. Jesus did this by rebuking the spirit of evil working through Peter, proclaiming, *"Get behind me, Satan! You are a stumbling block to me; you do not have in mind the concerns of God, but merely human concerns."* Matthew 16:21-23. After scolding Peter's spirit, Jesus also nurtured Peter's spirit, by inviting Peter to witness His Transfiguration (Matthew 17:1-4), to learn about the end times, e.g. entering the kingdom of God, sitting on twelve thrones, judging the twelve tribes of Israel. Meanwhile, Jesus instilled discipline in Peter, concerning earthly matters, e.g. paying taxes, and forgiving others.

6. *The Point is...Jesus will appoint you to a place & put you in it*

Jesus also allowed Peter to operate in his own strength, giving him opportune time to fail, fall, and suffer the guilt and shame of his own weakness. This occurred when Peter fell asleep in Gethsemane (Matthew 26), cut off the ear of the high priest's servant (Matthew 26:51), fearfully and unfaithfully followed Jesus at a distance when Jesus was arrested and (Matthew 26: 58), disowned Jesus three times before the rooster crowed. (Matthew 26: 75) Jesus restored Peter in the end and called him to service.

7. The Point is...Jesus will restore you after you fail, fall and suffer

When they came back from the tomb, they told all these things to the Eleven and to all the others. It was Mary Magdalene, Joanna, Mary the mother of James, and the others with them who told this to the apostles. But they did not believe the women, because their words seemed to them like nonsense. Peter, however, got up and ran to the tomb. Bending over, he saw the strips of linen lying by themselves, and he went away, wondering to himself what had happened. (Luke 24:9-12)

While the other disciples (apostles) did not believe the story of Mary, Joanna, and Mary, Peter struggled with his faith. Peter ran to the tomb to see for himself if Jesus was missing. Peter's faith was not a blind faith, it was informed with fact, filled with wonder and strengthened as he thought through the realities of who his savior was. Peter's faith was based on belief and not just blind acceptance. Peter needed to wrestle with his faith, to strengthen it!

8. The Point is...Jesus will call you to wrestle with your faith

Part 8 – Twenty Five (25) Tools in the Minister's Toolkit

"Relationships with People"

1. Be Relational - Build relationships with the people you plan to minister to. A mutually loving relationship keeps ministry alive.

2. Be Mutual - You are not the only Christian in the room. Don't treat others as though they need you to experience Jesus Christ.

3. Be Considerate - Don't minister to people until you irritate them. Learn to discern when people have experienced Jesus and when they've had enough of you.

4. Be Humble - Ministers are no greater than the people they serve. Remember Jesus said the greatest is the least of these.

"Pastoral Care & Visitations"

5. Be respectful - Remember that sick people may be very healthy spiritually. You may want to bless them but you will be blessed by them.

"Healing & Deliverance"

6. Be loving - Look to heal others with love. Point them to the Love of Jesus Christ as demonstrated on the cross.

7. Be Patient - Show others that deliverance can come in a moment, a minute or take a lifetime.

"Sowing & Reaping"

8. Be Perceptive - When you sow into others, you may not see the results right away. Sowers will often find rough terrain. Reapers may often find gorgeous landscapes that the Lord is beautifying.

"Preaching & Teaching"

9. Be Flexible - Learn to teach a little when you preach and preach a little after you teach. The gospel gives learning and burning to those yearning for life in Jesus Christ.

"Disciplines"

10. Be Proactive - Fast and pray for others. After you have invested in them in the heavenly realms, you will be helpful to them in the earthly realms.

11. Be Responsible - Commit to devotional time and bible study on your own time for yourself, and God will trust you with your own soul's salvation. Soon, God will entrust you to provide guidance, direction and oversight for others.

12. Be Mortal - As their leader you serve others with the towel and basin, but you should also learn to serve and fellowship with others as a team player. Since they've seen your divinity, you should let them see your humanity.

13. Be Surrendered - Praise and worship the Lord when you are alone and it will heighten the experience when you share it with others. Since you are dependent on the same God as them, you should share your adoration with them.

"Spiritual Maintenance"

14. Be Available - Keep learning about God and getting to know God. It requires prayer and study. It's like making a new best friend each day.

15. Be Enduring - Keep committing yourself to Jesus Christ and His church or the enemy will confuse your call and lead you to his amazingly disguised kingdom of darkness.

16. Be Attentive - Remember to treat the Scriptures as sacred. They will make you wise unto salvation. Overlook the words of God in your life and your quality of life dissipate with them.

17. Be Reciprocal - Keep getting and giving grace and mercy. Mercy is like shade in a deadly heat wave and grace is like a cold glass of water when it ends. You will need both to survive and recover from the heatwaves of life.

"Loving"

18. Be Consumed - Tie obedience to love. They require each other. Don't lie and suggest that you have one, or the other will reveal that it's not in you.

"Long Suffering"

19. Be Alert - Should you expect to receive only good from God? No, expect to suffer a little too. God doesn't spoil His children. He preserves us, by mixing in good and bad experiences.

20. Be Fillable - As Christ is daily filling you, watch the person of Jesus Christ be formed in you throughout your lifetime.

"Growing"

21. Be Balanced - What does it profit a man to inherit the world yet lose his own soul? Always balance the stuff that fills your life with the love of God that fills your heart. When your life is full of treasures but your heart is empty, you will know it's time to declutter your life and free up your heart.

22. Be Cultivated - What does it profit a man to walk in his calling yet decline in his character? You should be committed to growing as a person. Grow in character. Grow in integrity. Grow in quality of personality. Keep growing!

"Finding Balance"

23. Be Focused - Do not obsess over your calling. Only obsess over your God. God will keep calling and drawing you nearer. God will satisfy all of your urges, obsessions and callings.

24. Be Satisfied - Gifts, abilities, and ministries, are wonderful trophies to display but only God can fill you up and sustain you with His peace, presence and joy.

"Longevity"

25. Be Fresh - Stay young at heart. Enjoy the place, people, purpose, position, power, passion and presence that God bestows on you. If you only focus on the work, the problems, and the hard work required for the task at hand, it will kill you. Don't conform to a death sentence.

Part 9 - What you need to survive the call

To survive the call of God on your life it requires that you go on a journey. It's time to start packing. Let's look at the call of God on the life of Abraham and see what you will need. It's time to get focused!

Get "Destiny Focused" on your courage, expectation and purpose

Need #1 – You need courage to follow God

In (Deuteronomy 1:8), Moses says, "See, I have given you this land. Go in and take possession of the land the LORD swore he would give to your fathers—to Abraham, Isaac and Jacob—and to their descendants after them." God told Abraham that He would give him descendants as numerous as the starts in the sky. Then God led Abraham by faith to the promised Canaan land where these descendants live in the presence of God. Generations later, Abraham's great-grandson Joseph was sold into slavery, and taken to Egypt. After Joseph was freed from prison and rose in power, the rest of his Hebrew family left Canaan and followed Joseph to Egypt. The Hebrews remained in Egypt but were enslaved for 400 years. They called on God until God sent a deliverer, a man named Moses. Moses single handedly stood up to Pharaoh demanding that he release the prisoners, then he led them out of Egypt across the Red Sea in pursuit of the Promised Land.

Moses informed the children that it was time to go in and take possession of the land the Lord swore he would give to their fathers, to Abraham, Isaac, and Jacob and to their descendants after them. Then Moses told them that they were too heavy a burden for him to carry alone, because God had fulfilled his promise to Abraham. They were now as numerous as the stars in the sky, and they needed to choose some wise, understanding and respected men to be appointed as leaders over them.

Then as they left Horeb, and headed for the hill country of the Amorites, they reached Kadesh Barnea, Moses instructed them to go and take possession of the land as the Lord commanded. Moses told them to overcome fear and discouragement. Instead the Hebrew children asked to send spies to the land and bring back a report. Even Moses thought it was a good idea. The report was good. It was a good land that the Lord was giving them, but the Hebrews melted in fear. The people were stronger; the cities were larger, the walls were taller, and the Anakites were there. In that moment, they angered the Lord. The Lord called one man, Abraham to walk by faith. The Lord gave Abraham descendants as numerous as the stars in the sky. The Lord delivered them out of Egypt, led them by fire by night and cloud by day, he searched out places for them to camp, showed them the way, and led them the entire time. It was God who planned it all and prepared a bright future in mind for them. If they would only obey, God would lead them into the Promised Land, defeat their enemies and give them cities they wouldn't have to build.

Only if we had the courage to fear God and shun evil. We need courage to lead, courage to follow and courage to see the path. I've discovered many errors in their actions. If they had known the promise God made to Abraham, they would've known that they were the children of the promise that were as numerous as the stars in the sky.

When Moses told them to take the land, don't be afraid and don't be discouraged, they remained afraid and discouraged. Their plan to send spies was an act of fear! If they had courage they would've taken the land. Since they were discouraged, they wanted to send spies, and get a report of encouragement. The problem is that God gave them all of the encouragement they needed. God said go take the Land that I am giving you. Moses didn't reinforce the command that he gave them. Here, leadership, didn't hold them accountable to their charge. Moses should've made sure they went into the hill country. He let that bad idea pass. He lacked courage and succumbed to their wishes. He should've taken a yes or no. He should've required them to say yes we will go or no, we're afraid.

It's amazing how life is about yeses and nos. I was reading a book about the history of computers and it reminded me that all the complex technology today is built on 1s & 0s. At the binary level, a computer takes information, guidance and commands based on the arrangement of 1s & 0s. That's how it is with God, God can help us, lead us and guide us if we would only give him yeses and nos. Have the courage to choose. Courage will help you follow God and walk in your calling! Now, let's take a journey together to look at other tools you will need to survive the call of God!

Need #2 – You need to expect the best from God

Abraham left everything he owned to Isaac. But while he was still living, he gave gifts to the sons of his concubines and sent them away from his son Isaac to the land of the east. (Genesis 25:5-6 NIV)

This is the end of the journey for the father of faith, and the beginning of a new chapter for the promised son, or as we call him, Isaac, the son of the promise. As Abraham is preparing for death, he gave gifts to the sons of his concubines. They received their inheritance in the now (while Abraham was still living), unlike Isaac who would receive far greater later. They were sent away, distanced from the son of the promise, Isaac, so he could have space unhindered, so as not to disrupt his reign over his inherited estate.

Like sons without dads, or footsteps to trace, they were sent off to make a life of their own. It seems unfair to the sons of the concubines, but this is a clear picture of the clear path made for those who will walk in the faith versus the darkened, distant future reserved for those who will walk blindly through life without it.

If you are waiting to see what God has promised you, I implore you to look to your God who has etched out your path through life. Believe God when a glimpse of your future has been revealed to you. Know that God has an inheritance laid out for you and that God will clear out space for you to bask in God's blessings. Trust that each step will align you with the opportunities made available by God. Finally, expect God to grant you everything you need to live righteous and to leave a legacy of faithfulness for others to follow. Neil Armstrong became the first man to walk on the moon. He made one small step for man, and one giant leap for mankind. It was a long journey from earth to the moon and I'm sure they had faith as they left the earth's orbit, entered the lunar orbit, and landed on the moon. Like those brave men, keep walking by faith and reminding yourself that you will make it, your inheritance is soon to come.

Need #3 - You need to treasure your birthright

"Look, I am about to die," Esau said. "What good is the birthright to me?" (Genesis 25:32)

There's something about knowing what God wants. Abel gave an offering that pleased God. Rebekah knew that the older son would serve the younger. As she watched Esau hunting out in the open country while Jacob was at home among the tents and people, she knew that God had something special in mind for Jacob.

Many parents will tell their children that they are special once they will get a glimpse of what God is doing in their lives. There is no doubt that Rebekah told Jacob he would receive the blessing. Jacob knew when he asked Esau to sell his birthright for a bowl of stew (soup).

Esau didn't know how his future would pan out; furthermore, he didn't understand the heritage of being the first born son. He didn't know what pleased God. He sold his birthright and missed God's blessing, but Jacob seized the moment, aggressively pursued it and forsook all for the birthright which he knew was destined for him.

Do you know what God has for you? Has God given you a glimpse of your future? Do you have a spiritual sensitivity to God's will for you? Do you know what pleases God? Rebekah asked why the babies were fighting in her womb and God answered her. Esau never asked God what the birthright was good for. Today, I pray you ask what God has for you, what your future beholds, what pleases God!

Get "Spiritually Focused" on prayer and Transformation

Need #4 - You need to stop being anxious. Start praying!

Genesis 32:24 reads that *"So Jacob was left alone, and a man wrestled with him till daybreak."* NIV

Cheater, deceiver, liar, thief, betrayer, are all words that Esau could use to describe his brother Jacob who swindled Esau out of his birthright, and blessing. Tricked into cheap labor by his uncle, Jacob long-suffers for 20 years, but is developing integrity, a strong work ethic, and a genuine concern, love and respect for people and their possessions. Jacob is now returning home with his wives, children, servants, and livestock. He is now preparing to face his brother whom he tricked. Jacob is fearful for his life; for he enriched his own life at the expense of his brother's life. Jacob hurt Esau, who was betrayed and now lives with the reality that Jacob will live the life that was reserved for him. Nevertheless, Jacob steps up. He sends his family ahead. He now walks alone. No longer looking for blessings and possessions, he now seeks forgiveness, safety, security and shelter from retribution. God answers his prayer but greets him with a wrestling match. Jacob's struggling never ends. He is destined for blessing after blessing but is greeted with struggle after struggle.

What are you struggling with? Do you know that your struggle will lead to a blessing? Are you looking forward to your blessing or are you complaining about your struggles? Take this time to change your perspective! Cheer up! When the struggle is over, God's blessing will be revealed. God Bless!

Need #5 - You need to be transformed
(Dynamic, relational, complex)

"When Pharaoh calls you in and asks, 'What is your occupation?' you should answer, 'Your servants have tended livestock from our boyhood on, just as our fathers did.' Then you will be allowed to settle in the region of Goshen, for all shepherds are detestable to the Egyptians." (Genesis 46:33-34 NIV)

Here Joseph is a Hebrew that is sold into Egyptian slavery. He was put in charge of Egypt. He takes an Egyptian name, and wife. He sends for his family members who are in Canaan, but forewarns them and prepares them before meeting Pharaoh. He helps them get approval by Pharaoh to live in Goshen, near Egypt, despite that Egyptians detest Hebrews.

Joseph managed two identities, two worlds, two realities. What was Joseph's secret to living in 2 contrary cultures and while being a source of blessing to both? He'd been to the bottom where God was with him. When he arose to the top, God was with him. Whether at the top or bottom, God was with him and he helped everyone! Be available, useful, and dynamic, in any situation. **Be** relational with the people you are sent to help. Be capable of working with different types of people, in different places, and able to do different things wherever you are.

Get "Integrity Focused" on being fair and Rebuilt

Need #6 - You need to be fair privately and publicly

"When Pharaoh heard of this, he tried to kill Moses" (Exodus 2:15a)

Moses was in a difficult situation. While watching the Hebrew people at work, Moses saw an Egyptian beating a Hebrew. He killed the Egyptian. Word had gotten out. When Pharaoh heard, he tried to kill Moses, but Moses got away. Unbeknownst to him, Moses went from privately watching his people to privately defending his people. He would ultimately become the public deliverer of his people.

When God sees injustice, God may show you and invite you to bring justice and set His people free. Like Moses, you may find a new enemy and find your life under attack. Has God shown you someone that it is bondage, some situation that requires liberation or some blessing that needs to be released. Be careful for what you see. It may become your call to action! Remember that "Greater is he that is in you, than he that is in the world." (1 John 4:4) God Bless.

Need #7 - You need to come out!
(If God created a nation, God can rebuild you!)

"And I have promised to bring you up out of your misery in Egypt into the land of the Canaanites, Hittites, Amorites, Perizzites, Hivites and Jebusites---a land flowing with milk and honey." Exodus 3:17 NIV

There were Kings and nations that did not know God. And God knew this would happen. So God planned to reveal Himself to a man who would walk with God by faith and obey God. This man's obedience, and the legacy of faithful obedience passed down to each son would become the foundation of a nation that would be holy and righteous, belonging to The Lord God Jehovah. Despite their own negligence and outright rebellion toward God, He still brought them out of their misery over and over again!

Why are you still imprisoned in self-doubt, despair, and confusion? If God can build a new unsuspecting nation of Priests and Kings from one faithful person, then why can't God bring you out and set you up for success?

Get "Relationally Focused" on worship, communication & help

Need #8 - You need to worship the Lord your God

But Moses said to God, "Who am I that I should go to Pharaoh and bring the Israelites out of Egypt?" And God said, "I will be with you. And this will be the sign to you that it is I who have sent you: When you have brought the people out of Egypt, you will worship God on this mountain." (Exodus 3:11-12 NIV)

Called to liberate the Israelites from Egypt, Moses asked God who am I to do this. In other words, why are you sending me? Here Moses is filled with fear and doubt. Like many of us, Moses tries to understand how and why God would use him. Moses wants God to assure him that he is qualified for the job. But here is the problem.

Moses is not qualified to do the job. God is qualified though! God promises to be with Moses. God's only reassurance is a sign. Here's the sign. When you leave Egypt, you will worship me. That's not a sign to inspire or encourage you; that's a sign to remind you. Note to self, God will be with you to help you get the job done, but remember to worship The Lord, your God before the people. Acknowledge his goodness and unmerited favor that is at work in you. Let everyone see that it is God behind it all!

Need #9 - You need to talk to God
About your assignment

He will speak to the people for you, and it will be as if he were your mouth and as if you were God to him. (Exodus 4:16 NIV)

The creator of the universe sent the prophetic preacher and liberator of the Hebrew slaves to Pharaoh with a word from God to let God's people go. As God was speaking to Moses, Moses started making excuses. His statements began with "but what if...," and "pardon your servant but I am not..." Moses started making excuses because Moses felt ill equipped to influence them, convince them that God spoke to him, to describe his God if necessary, or to speak confidently and eloquently to them.

Here's how wonderful God was to Moses. God anticipated Moses' excuses. He taught Moses a few miraculous signs to gain influence. He provided an assistant (Aaron) to do the talking and He offered to teach Moses and Aaron what to say and what to do. God taught Moses a great lesson that all great leaders must learn...how to depend on God for direction and to delegate what he was incapable of doing.

In all of this, Moses learned trust God. God could have used someone else, but God was totally dedicated and committed to using, growing and maturing Moses in the same way God is committed to using, growing and maturing you. Are you ready for the challenge that God has for you? You won't get to God's provisions until you and God talk about your assignment. Endure!

Need #10 - You need to welcome the right hand of God

Your right hand, Lord, was majestic in power. Your right hand, Lord, shattered the enemy. (Exodus 15:6)

After God defeated the Egyptians for Moses and the Israelites, Moses & his sister Miriam broke out into a song of praise, celebrating the power in the right hand of God. They knew that only God could save them. They lived according to God's mercy and they watched God deliver them in time of need.

I'm amazed at how quickly I try to fight my own battles and ignore my God who is watching over me, prepared to shatter the enemy with His right hand because the battle is really His. What if I didn't get in the way? What if I waited on The Lord and merely watched Him at work. I believe the battles would end sooner, the struggle would subside, and there would be no scar. The next time I am trapped between an army and a sea, I will lift mine eyes unto the hills and look for my help because the right hand of The Lord will surely destroy my enemies!

Get "Situationally Focused" On God's Day, God's process & God's promise

Need #11 - You need to obey God on the Sabbath

"...the Lord has given you the Sabbath; that is why on the sixth day he gives you bread for two days. Everyone is to stay where they are on the seventh day; no one is to go out." (Exodus 16:27-30 NIV)

God created the world in six days but on day seven, God said it was good. God rested and called that day the Sabbath. He created it for us, so we would rest also. Is it rest from labor? Is it rest in God? It is rest for your flesh to let your soul enjoy God's blessing. In exodus 16, God provided manna for the hungry travelers 6 days a week, and double on 6th day so they wouldn't have to gather it on the Sabbath. They disobeyed. How often does God provide and we miss God totally? Oh how destructive is the lack of understanding, lack of faith, direct disdain and disobedience to God's commands. Our leadership, ourselves and our peer communities are all held accountable when we sin!

Need #12 - You need to reverence the Process

Moses' father-in-law replied, "What you are doing is not good. You and these people who come to you will only wear yourselves out. The work is too heavy for you; you cannot handle it alone. (Exodus 18:17-18 NIV)

God gave Moses the law, but God also gave Jethro a word. Moses had to surrender his leadership style, and his people's dependence on him. This 40-year wilderness journey has a lot to teach us today. It's a cycle and it's all about timing. Get filled for the journey, follow the Lord, and enjoy his blessing when someone else has a word!

Need #13 - You need to hold onto His promise

Now if you obey me fully and keep my covenant, then out of all nations you will be my treasured possession. Although the whole earth is mine, you will be for me a kingdom of priests and a holy nation.' These are the words you are to speak to the Israelites." (Exodus 19:5-6 NIV)

After God delivered the Hebrews from Egypt, God led them to Mt. Sinai. As they were approaching Mt Sinai, the Lord extended Himself to them, offering a relationship and a promise. The promise was that if they keep God's covenant and obey God's commands fully, they would become God's treasured possession, a kingdom of priests, a Holy Nation. Oh what a promise. Imagine that you are favored by God, chosen to minister to God through worship. Well, God has chosen you. God has plans for you to be different, set apart, separated, renewed and transformed into a new creation that is acceptable and pleasing to God.

If you are too afraid, indifferent, ashamed, or simply unprepared to accept God's invitation, then pray for a glimpse of God's promise. Hold onto the hope of God's promise. There's no room for both hope and fear.

Get "Commitment Focused" on what you say and do

Need #14 - You need to watch what you say!

"Do not blaspheme God or curse the ruler of your people." (Exodus 22:28 NIV)

As they journey from Egypt to the Promised Land, Israel is preparing to become the new powerhouse nation. Moses is teaching Israel how to function as its own nation, solely dependent on God. To engage with other nations, Israel must remember who their God is. The people must remain loyal and committed to their deliverer. Their survival, success, and sustainment depend on their obedience and dependence on God. The same goes for believers today. You must remain loyal and committed to God in everything you do and say No, dishonorable, rebellious, or ungrateful talk is allowed! Go represent your God, your God appointed leadership and your liberty in Christ! Express your undying faith, love, devotion and allegiance to your God from your heart. Your words will honor God!

Need #15 - You need to setup the Tabernacle

The Lord said to Moses, "Tell the Israelites to bring me an offering. You are to receive the offering for me from everyone whose heart prompts them to give. These are the offerings you are to receive from them: gold, silver and bronze; blue, purple and scarlet yarn and fine linen; goat hair; ram skins dyed red and another type of durable leather; acacia wood; olive oil for the light; spices for the anointing oil and for the fragrant incense; and onyx stones and other gems to be mounted on the ephod and breast piece. Set up the tabernacle according to the plan shown you on the mountain. (Exodus 25:1-7, 26:30 NIV)

God wanted to be present with his community of believers, so God called Moses to the mountain and gave him the plan for building a Tabernacle to house God's presence. Then God asked for an offering from everyone whose heart prompted them to give. The people didn't know it but the gold, silver, bronze, yarn, linen, skins, wood, oil, spices, and gems they offered were all used to build the tabernacle. Together, their offerings became God's house. No offering, no house. What are you offering god? Do you offer God praise? You know and God inhabits the praises of His people. Do you offer your life as a living sacrifice, holy and acceptable unto God? You know God can use you if you have been crucified with Christ, and resurrected by His spirit. Do you love The Lord your God and love your neighbor as you love yourself? The bible says that God is love and when you love others, you give them the opportunity to experience God. Give God an offering today, and a place to tabernacle in your life!

Get

"Purity Focused"

on

God's presence,

God's sacredness

&

God's anointing

Need #16 - You need to make room for God

"Then I will dwell among the Israelites and be their God. They will know that I am the Lord their God, who brought them out of Egypt so that I might dwell among them. I am the Lord their God." (Exodus 29:45-46 NIV)

We have a God who spoke creation into being, formed man from the dust of the ground. Then called a nation out of one man, Abraham, delivered them from bondage in Egypt and led them to their promised land. Still today, that same God longs to be with us, to know us intimately and personally, to be our God and to be recognized as such. Do you know your God? Does God dwell with you? Is there room for God in your life? Remember to make room for your deliverer to dwell with you after he rescues you from bondage. You are like a home set for demolition that was rescued, restored and sold to the highest bidder, and your buyer is God! Enjoy your purchaser!

Need #17 - You need to be Sacred

Take the following fine spices...Make these into a sacred anointing oil...Anoint Aaron and his sons and consecrate them so they may serve me as priests...Say to the Israelites, 'Do not pour it on anyone else's body and do not make any other oil using the same formula. It is sacred, and you are to consider it sacred. (Exodus 30:23, 25, 30-32 NIV)

God says you are sacred to me. You are the perfume I choose to smell. Longing for the holy aroma to arise out of you. God has plans for His people to make love offerings, sacrifices and acts of obedience to God. God wants His people set aside for Him, consecrated to be used in His service, for His glory, to serve His will. He anoints us with Holy oil and declares that we are the sacred vessels to be used. The oil is Holy; for God says so. The vessel is holy, chosen by God. The service of The Lord is holy, a life lived to glorify God!

Don't misuse what God says is holy, neither His formula for making holy oil, nor the holy oil, nor the person who is to be used by God.

Need #18 - You need to know you are anointed to tell the world!

Then the LORD said to Moses, ² "See, I have chosen Bezalel son of Uri, the son of Hur, of the tribe of Judah, ³ and I have filled him with the Spirit of God, with wisdom, with understanding, with knowledge and with all kinds of skills— ⁴ to make artistic designs for work in gold, silver and bronze, ⁵ to cut and set stones, to work in wood, and to engage in all kinds of crafts. (Exodus 31:1-5 NIV)

The anointing is not what you think. God does not fill you with the spirit just to make you feel good, or to make you shout. The spirit empowers you to fulfill the will of God. When God was ready to build the tabernacle and everything in it, God filled a man with the spirit, with wisdom, understanding, knowledge and various skills to work with precious stones, metals, crafts and to make artistic designs. He was from the tribe of Judah. Just think a man born to praise God, yet skilled with his hands, a master at work. Some say you can testify without saying a word, because your life will tell it all. Well, you can praise God through the excellence of your labor and show that God is worthy.

Get

"Devotionally Focused"

on your love, longing

and looking

Need #19 - You need to love God and Man

Why should the Egyptians say, 'It was with evil intent that he brought them out, to kill them in the mountains and to wipe them off the face of the earth'? Turn from your fierce anger; relent and do not bring disaster on your people. (Exodus 32:12)

While Moses was talking with God, learning the law, having the law written on tablets of stone by the finger of God, the Hebrew people were at the bottom of the mountain losing patience, falling into sin and revelry. God planned to destroy them, but Moses found favor with God. He convinced God that God should not destroy them because God would destroy His own reputation with them. Oh that someone cared for God!?! In one breath, Moses expressed deep concern for both God and His people: God who deserves recognition and glory; man who deserves punishment for sin. The Law requires us to love God and man. Moses bore the law in his hands when He convinced God not to destroy them. He also bore it in his heart. Where does your love lie?

Need #20 - You need to long for more of God.

If you are pleased with me, teach me your ways so I may know you and continue to find favor with you...The Lord replied, "My Presence will go with you, and I will give you rest." (Exodus 33:13a-14)

Our ways are not God's ways. God wants to instill Himself and His ways into us. This was evident in the incarnation of Christ and the indwelling of the Holy Spirit. God has done His part to indicate this. For our part, we need to yield to God, to humbly and faithfully follow God's leading in our lives. Then God will determine if God is pleased with us, and if so, God will draw nearer to us. In doing so, we will rest in the presence of God and learn God's ways. By yielding, we get more out of God!

Need #21 - You need to watch God work amazing wonders

Although this is a stiff-necked people, forgive our wickedness and our sin, and take us as your inheritance." Then the Lord said: "I am making a covenant with you. Before all your people I will do wonders never before done in any nation in all the world. The people you live among will see how awesome is the work that I, the Lord, will do for you. (Exodus 34:9b-10)

Despite their sinful sickness, God Covenanted His people and did wonders before their eyes, wonders that He had never done before. God is still doing wonders today for His people. The church's cup is running over with blessing. If we could look down from Heaven and see what God sees and see how God is moving in His churches and moving through the lives of His people, it would blow our minds. God is doing amazing things. See the magnificence of God by watching what God is doing. Don't doubt or deny God. Don't let your sin and self-centeredness stop you from seeing what God is doing. He will draw you into a great work if you are open and receptive to Him!

Get "Consecration-ally Focused" on being helpful, holy & obedient

Need #22- You need to help in building the sanctuary

Then Moses summoned Bezalel and Oholiab and every skilled person to whom the Lord had given ability and who was willing to come and do the work. They received from Moses all the offerings the Israelites had brought to carry out the work of constructing the sanctuary. And the people continued to bring freewill offerings morning after morning. So all the skilled workers who were doing all the work on the sanctuary left what they were doing and said to Moses, "The people are bringing more than enough for doing the work the Lord commanded to be done." (Exodus 36:2-5 NIV)

The Lord commanded the Israelites give offerings and help build the sanctuary. Each morning, the Israelites brought offerings, so many that the skilled workers stopped working and asked Moses to tell the people to stop giving because they gave too many offerings. Imagine if the church today could see what God was doing in our midst. What if we were so enthusiastic by what God was doing that we bought in to it and sold out for it.

Need #23 – You need to be holy!
God is already working on you

Leviticus 21:8 says, *"Regard them as holy, because they offer up the food of your God. Consider them holy, because I the Lord am holy---I who make you holy."* NIV It is a basic truth that our God is holy. What He does is holy. The children he creates are made holy. The ones who are drawn near to serve Him are holy. Consider them holy and treat them as such. When you see them, remember that God made them different, separated for God's service just as God made you, holy, separated unto The Lord for great works of service.

Even in Leviticus 15:31, God instructs, "You must keep the Israelites separate from things that make them unclean, so they will not die in their uncleanness for defiling my dwelling place, which is among them." In contemporary, vernacular, and in New Testament theology, that would be, stay clean my friend. You must be clean to enter my presence.

Need #24 - You need to obey God. It's hard but required

"You must not offer to the Lord an animal whose testicles are bruised, crushed, torn or cut. You must not do this in your own land, and you must not accept such animals from the hand of a foreigner and offer them as the food of your God. They will not be accepted on your behalf, because they are deformed and have defects." (Leviticus 22:24-25 NIV)

Obedience is better than sacrifice! God establishes the rules and guidelines that we all must obey. God establishes his people on them, and we develop and mature in obedience to god's commands. In Leviticus 22:24-25, God says certain animals with certain deformities were not acceptable by God. Israelites could not accept them from foreigners, nor use them for sacrificial offerings. God has set the standard and we cannot violate it. God expects the best. God wants us to accept only the best.

Part 10 - You need to Testify

Get "Accountability Focused" and Ready to go testify!

You know, the more we read the bible, the more we discover what we are being held accountable for doing.

Leviticus 5:1 for example, reads that "If anyone sins because they do not speak up when they hear a public charge to testify regarding something they have seen or learned about, they will be held responsible." Yes, God has great expectations for His children. There are many behaviors that God wants us to overcome. Sin is more than abusive drinking, doing drugs or using foul language. God is calling us to do more than what comes to us naturally. God is calling us to the spirit of love, high moral character, and the spirit of integrity. So we will express outwardly what has been deposited into our spirits internally.

Leviticus 5 tells us that when the community makes a public charge against someone about something, we are to speak up and testify if we have seen or heard something about it. It amazes me that as God was building the community of faith, a God still cared for the community at large. And if a God cares for His community of people still large, He must care for each and every one of us. For example, if I steal from my neighbor, and you see it, God wants you to speak up and tell somebody about the sin you witnessed. But then on the other hand, if I am being blamed for stealing something, and you know I didn't do it, you should speak up and tell somebody.

Now, if you don't speak up and testify then God calls that sin. Remember God was building a community of believers, and He needed them to develop character and integrity. God is still developing His community of faith, and God is still calling us to testify! The world today believes there is a God and some even believe in God. But most of us don't believe in Jesus Christ, won't surrender our lives to follow Christ, and most definitely won't testify on behalf of Jesus, the Christ!

On the other hand, if you won't testify about the Lord, Jesus Christ, then go ahead and stay in your sin!

- In John 1:15, John the Baptist came and testified 'He who comes after me has surpassed me because he was before me.
- In john 1:34, John the Baptist declared that "I have seen, and I testify that this is God's Chosen One."
- When Jesus was getting baptized In Mathew 3:17, the father said, "This is my Son, whom I love; with him I am well pleased."
- In John 15:26, Jesus told John, "When the Advocate comes, He will testify about me.
- When Jesus entered Jerusalem and the disciples were praising Him, Jesus said, "I tell you…if they keep quiet, the stones will cry out." Luke 19:40
- St John the Apostle testified to the things Jesus did and wrote them down.
- When the Jews dragged Jesus away to Pilate, Pilate said "I find no basis for a charge against this man."
- When Pilate sent Jesus to Herod, The chief priests and teachers of the law were accusing Jesus, Herod and his soldiers ridiculed him and sent him back to Pilate. Luke 23:10-11

No one wanted to testify about Jesus! Pilate wanted to testify on behalf of Jesus and release Him, but the crowds said crucify Him. They punished Jesus, beat Him all night long, and nailed Him to an old wooden cross. He died for your sins and mine. After 3 days He rose from that grave. And the question remains, will you testify now? Will you tell somebody that I am God! That them that I love you with an everlasting love that I am the alpha and omega. The beginning and the end, the way, the truth and the light! Will you tell somebody that God wants to walk with you and talk with you and tell you that you belong to Him!

FOLLOW THE LORD JESUS

AND

SURVIVE THE CALL OF GOD!

Part 11 – Reminder to Survive the Call

Remember that God reveals Himself to us and walks with us. At some point in the journey, God calls us to obedience, revealing to us that God is holy and we are sinful. God challenges us to ultimately confront ourselves, seeing ourselves in the light of His presence, in our actual context. Then God reveals the setup to us. We have to go through to get through. We have to sojourn through the call to walk into our ministry.

The Apostle Peter endured such a journey. Peter had to learn to submit to Jesus. Becoming someone else's servant was an arduous task for Peter. Becoming someone else's fruit, having his life interrupted and seeing his life joined to a greater plan was discomforting. It was intrusive. God doesn't force you to submit. On the contrary, God compels you to submit. God inspires you to surrender yourself to Him, allowing your life to be used for a greater purpose. As Peter surrendered, Jesus took the reins of Peter's heart, performing miracles for Peter as He did others, to ignite their belief. Jesus empowers His believers, Jesus plants His followers so they will discover their assignment, understand their power and act within their boundaries. For, our God is a God who instills boundaries so there is structure and order. Though God's spirit moves beyond the boundaries and structured order to accomplish necessary and impossible feats, God uses the boundaries for our protection. Though Peter failed his tests, and suffered, he ultimately wrestled with his faith and grew stronger in it.

You too will wrestle with your call. You will need courage to follow God, enough courage to look for God, to see God in your future, to see a bright future for you, even in the context of your calling. So, expect God to do immeasurably more than you can ask or think. Value and appreciate what God is giving you. Trust God for preparing a unique life and a wonderful plan for bringing it to pass. Pray yourself into the place of gratitude. As you see each challenge coming, as you face each distraction to your faith, be shrewd enough to see trouble for what it is. Be flexible and dynamic; be complex and discerning. Transform from being called to be filled with truth and emptied out in service to others.

Though the journey is long, and each goal along the journey seems out of reach, I encourage you to be steadfast. Keep praying and refuse anxiety. Treat others the way you expect to be treated when God shows up and blesses you with ministry opportunities. I urge you to be fair with others, both privately and publicly. Always watch God at work. God is still doing amazing wonders, and you are called to testify to His wonders! You are anointed to tell the world!

When times get rough, talk to God about your assignment, only God can fix it. Remain obedient to God. Though it is hard to be obedient sometimes and it is difficult to understand why God wants you to do certain things, it is still required. Continue to walk in holiness, long for more of the God who is changing you. Chasten yourself to love God and Man, and continue to yield to God, making room for Him in your life until you find yourself saturated with His presence, His will, His liberty to correct you and refocus you. Reverence the process that God put you in. Hold on to God's promise and be careful for what you say that you don't cast off your faith in God with words from your mouth.

ABOUT THE AUTHOR

Dr. Derrick L Randolph, Sr. is from Baltimore, Maryland.

www.ingramcontent.com/pod-product-compliance
Lightning Source LLC
Chambersburg PA
CBHW060417050426
42449CB00009B/2005